Sketch of the Life

OF

ELDER HUMPHREY POSEY,

FIRST BAPTIST MISSIONARY
TO THE CHEROKEE INDIANS, AND FOUNDER OF VALLEY
TOWN SCHOOL, NORTH CAROLINA.

BY ROBERT FLEMING,

OF NEWNAN, GEORGIA.

Republished by
The Old Paths Publications, Inc.
www.theoldpathspublications.com
TOP@theoldpathspublications.com
NOVEMEMBER 2019
ISBN: 978-1-7341927-2-8

PUBLISHED BY THE
WESTERN BAPTIST ASSOCIATION OF GEORGIA.
1852.

KING & BAIRD, Printers,
   Sansom St., Philadelphia.

NOTICE.

This very brief Memoir of Elder Posey, has been prepared by the Author, at the request of the Western Baptist Association, Georgia. It is hoped that the numerous friends of the deceased may be interested in its perusal, and that the religion of Christ may be promoted by its circulation. But it is especially hoped, that the cause of Indian Missions may be aided, and the general cause of benevolence subserved.

CONTENTS.

	PAGE
PRELIMINARY REMARKS..	7

CHAPTER I.

Birth of Humphrey Posey.—His Education.—Habits of Early Life. 13

CHAPTER II.

His Marriage.—Conversion.—Impressions on Preaching.—Ordination... 19

CHAPTER III.

Revival of the Missionary Cause in Europe.—Among the Baptists in America.—American Board of Commissioners.—Triennial Convention.—Valley Town Mission among the Cherokee Indians.—Mr. Posey's Agency and Influence among them..................... 32

CHAPTER IV.

Character of Elder Posey as a Christian.—A Preacher.—A Pastor.—A Yoke-fellow in the Ministry.—Letter from Elder A. Webb.—Interesting Anecdote.—Dr. Howell's Letter.—Respect of the Indians for him. 67

CONTENTS.

CHAPTER V.

PAGE

The Organization of the Georgia Baptist Convention.—Presence of Elder Posey.—His Labors in Georgia.—Agency for Cave Spring School, in Floyd County.—Death of Mrs. Posey.—His Marriage to Mrs. Jane Stokes, and Settlement in Newnan.—His Death. 85

CHAPTER VI.

Persecution of Elder Posey.—Anecdote.—Method of Preaching.—His Portrait. 93

PRELIMINARY REMARKS.

From the days of John the Baptist until now, the Baptists have been more famous for preaching in the wilderness, than for wearing soft raiment, and for dwelling in king's houses. They have generally been looked upon as reeds shaken with the wind, and have every where been spoken against. Many of them have been eloquent ministers of Jesus Christ, "fervent in the spirit, and mighty in the scriptures," and have "taught diligently the things of the Lord." Some of the most distinguished men which the world has ever known were in principle and profession Baptists. A record of their history has not, however, in all instances, been preserved. In this respect, the Baptists have not done justice to themselves nor to the cause they so heartily adhere to. They have probably been criminal in this thing to a greater extent than they are able to perceive. The great, and almost unparalleled increase of their numbers within the past and present century, has given rise to an era in their history which will, no doubt, mark their general character for centuries to come.

The establishment of "*The American Baptist Publication Society*" will be remembered. Through it the enlightened world may learn what the Baptists were, what they now are, and what they probably will be. But while the pages of their general history are rapidly assuming a more interesting aspect, will not the department of biography add largely to the amount of pleasure and improvement of the thoughtful, candid reader? Almost all classes feel interested in perusing biographical sketches of remarkable persons. There is a kind of charm in this department of literature, which is rarely found in any other species of history. "Many valuable observations in the conduct of human life," says a good writer, in the

Encyclopedia of Religious Knowledge, " may be made from the accounts of those who have been eminent and useful in the world." Indeed, the lives of wicked persons often furnish us with lessons of instruction. They point with certainty to the fatal consequences which, sooner or later, follow a life of heedlessness and rebellion against God. We may not be able to derive pleasure from perusing the sketches of an unholy life, and therefore may not feel anxious to perpetuate the memory of those who have contributed to augment the sum of human woe. Yet there still lingers in our fallen nature, it would seem, a universal consent that "*the remembrance of the wicked shall perish from the earth, and he shall have no name in the street.*" Job xviii. 17. But while "the name of the wicked shall rot" in forgetfulness, "*the memory of the just is blessed.*" Prov. x. 7. It is a debt we owe to the memory of those who have given their time, their talents, and their lives to promote the best interests of our bodies and souls.

This world has often been termed a wilderness. Holy writ declares we are "travelers and sojourners, as all our fathers were." It would, therefore, seem that it may be a good work to write a good biography of a good man,—to delineate the journey through this wilderness, and sketch the more useful parts for the benefit of those who may come after. Thus the young traveler may learn how to take advantage of the rough and disastrous places which he may have to encounter. He may also learn how to avoid the dangerous precipices over which his predecessors have been incautiously precipitated.

In attempting to give a sketch of the life of Elder Posey, the writer considers himself called upon, from a variety of considerations, to inform the reader, at the outset, that he is fully sensible of his inability to give to his friends that kind of production which they are desirous to see, and which they have a right, in some degree, to demand. The incidents in his life, from the mere circumstance of his locality in the missionary field, were many and interesting. But a record of them has not been preserved, and but few, comparatively, can now be collected for the benefit of surviving friends. To gather up his numerous religious letters on business connected with his missionary career, is impossible; and his private correspondence, though somewhat extensive, has not been in many instances preserved. His diary of travels through various parts of our country, is disconnected, and of such a character as to be of little service in preparing this sketch. From what his friends have known of him, and from what the writer has obtained by the assistance of some of his worthy acquaintances and fellow-laborers in the gospel ministry, he hopes to give a history of this excellent servant of the Lord, which will be interesting and useful to those who know how to appreciate plain productions, and who desire truth, more than embellishment, in works of this kind.

The sketch of the rise and progress of

Modern Missions in Europe and America, given in the third chapter of this work, seemed indispensable. Many valuable histories of Missions have issued from the press; but who read them and where are they to be found? It is a lamentable fact, that many of our good brethren in the ministry have never seen such books as "*Choules' History of Missions,*" or "*Gammells,*" or even the little tract called "*History of the Burman Mission.*" It is hoped that the short account given in these pages, will be very acceptable to those who may not possess the works alluded to above. Posey's life was so identified with the cause of Missions, that it was impossible to give his history without giving some detailed account of the Missionary operations amongst us.

CHAPTER I.

Birth of Humphrey Posey.—Education.—Habits of early life.

Elder Humphrey Posey was born in Henry County, Virginia, January 12th, 1780. When he was about five years old, his father removed to Burke County, North Carolina, where young Posey spent his childhood and youth. He was blessed with parents who felt it to be their duty to bring up their children in the nurture and admonition of the Lord. His mother had been a member of the Church of Jesus Christ from her youth, and was, we are informed, a woman of considerable reading, and of very strong mind. But, best of all, she was possessed of high-toned piety. She was not merely a Baptist by profession, her head and her heart were sound in God's statutes; and she was a woman of true

Christian decision. This last mentioned trait in her character, her son Humphrey inherited in an uncommon degree. He was almost a stranger to vacillation and suspense in the performance of either his religious or secular duties. His mind, like his body, never lingered in its movements. His mother taught him, when but a child, having no spelling book, to spell and read in the Psalter; and by the time he was seven years old, he had read through the New Testament several times, without the opportunity of going to school more than twenty days. Might we not pause here for a moment to inquire whether the hand of the Lord may not be distinctly seen in this early period, shaping, through maternal instrumentality, the mind and character of this poor and obscure boy, for the great work whereunto he was afterwards called. May we not also see how the mind, like the body, becomes strong and active by early well-directed exercise. It is a fact not unworthy of notice, that Elder Posey had an excellent memory, and he was remarkably familiar with the word of God, which he had treasured up in his heart when he was a child; and when he was old it had not departed from him.

He was not what is usually called an educated man, having never attended school more than to enable him to read, write, and perform the simple rules of arithmetic. He never, at school, studied English grammar. He commenced teaching "*little old-field schools,*" as he used to call them, when about seventeen years old. And as he who teaches, learns faster than he who is being taught, so it was with young Posey. He had a great thirst for knowledge. Holy writ assures us, "Through desire a man having separated himself, seeketh and intermeddleth with all wisdom." Prov. xviii. 1. This Bible truth is very strikingly illustrated in his case; for he became what may be termed a good English scholar. He wrote and spelled well, pronounced accurately, spoke grammatically, thought clearly, and reasoned forcibly. He possessed enough of good common sense to keep him, however, from setting himself up as competent to criticise the language and pronunciation of those who had claims to scholarship. Nor was he spoiled by that disgusting dogmatism and self-importance which are so frequently found in ruinous connection with those who are self-taught and self-made, and who have acquired without merit a kind of popularity amongst their fellows. It is probably true, in some instances, that "a little learning is a dangerous thing"; but it is certainly a shallow mind that is intoxicated by shallow draughts.

He was fond of vocal music, and was well acquainted with the principles of that science. When young, his voice was very good, and, "singing with the spirit and with the understanding also," he had great power over his congregations. How desirable that a minister should possess this gift, and cultivate it!

In his person, Elder Posey was over the ordinary size of men; with fair complexion, and clear blue eyes, he might be considered handsome. But he was more than this; he was dignified and commanding in his personal appearance,—always easy and affable in his intercourse with others,—never phlegmatic nor morose.

Many young men of the present day, should they ever cast an eye over these pages, will probably be surprised to find that with opportunities so poor he should rise to so much distinction. But in reference to difficulties, it may be truly said of him—

"Where some see mountains, he but atoms sees."

Naturalists tell us that the wings of the ostrich are not adapted to flying. Their structure authorizes the conclusion, and facts establish it—*the ostrich cannot fly.* So it is with some minds; they cannot rise above difficulties—never can expand, nor mount, nor soar. But the kind Creator gave the subject of this biographical notice a mind of superior make—fitted for almost any exigency. Fixed in its purpose, it grasped and mastered whatever came within its reach. Having to "work for a living," his body and his mind were both greatly benefited. The one was healthful and vigorous, the other clear, active, and energetic. No dull nor sluggish movements characterized neither the one nor the other. Indeed, his soul and his body seemed to be made for each other.

CHAPTER II.

His Marriage.—Conversion.—Impressions on preaching.—His Ordination.

The subject of this Memoir was a few days more than twenty years old when he married. This marriage would not be considered by Dr. Franklin a misfortune; though some green philosophers of the present age might deprecate early marriages. He selected a pious wife, though himself, at that time, not professing to be a converted man. He believed the Bible was a revelation from God, and he acted upon that belief. As a lover of wisdom, he sought a wife of whom he could say, "She openeth her mouth with wisdom, and in her tongue is the law of kindness." Prov. xxxi. 26. A sensible man will always endeavor to select such a wife. "She will do him good, and not evil, all the days of her life." Prov. xxxi. 12.

Among the papers left by Elder Posey, is found, in his own handwriting, a brief account of his religious experience. It will be proper to give the reader this account just as he has left it, that he may have a correct specimen of his style in writing; while it will exhibit his views of the work of the Holy Spirit upon his heart in an interesting and instructive manner. He says:—

"My parents taught me very early the danger of sin, and I had serious thoughts about a future state when very young. Sometimes I was afraid to go to sleep, on account of the dread I had of the judgment's coming and finding me unprepared; and I was often terrified with dreams, so that I never could be said to enjoy fully 'the pleasures of sin.' Still, I put off seeking the salvation of my soul until I was about eighteen years old. I often promised to reform, but I as often broke my vows. Now the subject was brought home to my conscience with so much power, that I began to retire into secret places to pray —became very much dejected, but in a short time my distress left me, and I became quite calm. This continued several years, during which time I never could allow myself to go into open sin, (and I will here state that I was preserved, somehow, so that I never swore a profane oath in my life, to my knowledge,) but still my mind was carnal. At about seventeen years of age, I began teaching 'little old-field schools,' and also vocal music, in Greenville District, South Carolina. In the Spring of 1799, I went into Union District to follow the same occupation. On the 28th day of January, 1800, I was united in marriage with Lettice Jolly, then a pious member of the Methodist Episcopal Church. I taught school, that year, in the same community, and in 1801 removed into Greenville District. All this while my mind was occasionally deeply affected. Some time about the end of this year, after I had gone to bed, I fell into a doze, and I was addressed so plainly, that I rose hastily up in my bed, believing some human being had spoken to me in these words: '*Without you repent carefully you shall die, but if you repent there is yet mercy for you.*' I studied the expression, and believed it was from the Lord, and that it was the last call I should be favored with, and I determined immediately to set about the work. I commenced trying to pray, but could not regulate my mind, nor feel any tenderness—*not a tear could I shed.* I began now to feel the corruption of my nature, and the deceitfulness of my heart. I feared greatly that I had sinned away my day of grace, and that now there was no mercy for me. I could see how Christ could save others, but mine was a peculiar case. I could not do any thing at all in the right way. I could not mourn for sin *right*, nor *pray right;* and *every* effort I made seemed to plunge me deeper into the mire. This state of feeling continued nearly a month, and I went to a Baptist meeting, on the Lord's-day, when, to my surprise, a large congregation was in attendance, and singing; which had not been the case there for a long time previous. It struck me there would be a revival, and I went in under very solemn impressions. There were two sermons preached, with no apparent effect; but when the preaching was closed, a Presbyterian gentleman, by request, got up and described a camp-meeting which he had attended just previous to this, and which was, probably, the first in the State. The description was given in such a manner that it affected the whole congregation, and my hard heart was softened, so that I shed tears freely. A lively exhortation ensued, and an invitation to seekers being given, I was probably the first to go forward to give the preacher my hand to be prayed for. I was glad that I could weep, and I felt that I would rather stay *right there* than to go home; but still I could not think that my sins were forgiven. But I could now pray with some fervor, and therefore hoped there was yet mercy for me. I went home, and my sadness increased. In the morning I took up the hymn-book, and commenced singing the hymn beginning—

   'How happy are they
    Who their Saviour obey,' &c.

"I thought they were the happiest people in the world; but here was I, *a sinner*, who had no part in it. I laid down the book and retired for secret prayer, which, I think, I engaged in about four times that night; but found no relief. This struggle continued about four days and nights, during which time sins that had been long committed came fresh to my recollection. I felt that I was in the worst condition of any sinner, *mainly* on account of the badness of my heart. I thought I was not fit to be on this earth, and acknowledged from my *heart* that if God should send me to hell it would be just, and I could not see how he could be just and save me. My anguish was past expression. About the fourth night, I went almost in despair, and kneeled down by a pile of rocks in my field, and having found so many evils in my heart, and not willing to remain in ignorance of my real character, I begged the Lord to show me the worst of my case, and if there was mercy in store for such a hell-deserving wretch, for the dear Redeemer's sake, to let it be bestowed. In this agony, light broke into my soul, with an impression like this, '*Thy sins are forgiven thee.*' My soul was filled with joy, and it appeared to me astonishing that I had not sooner discovered the way of salvation through Jesus Christ. My mind was now drawn out for the salvation of sinners.* I thought I could tell them so plainly the way, that they would certainly believe and be saved. But notwithstanding I could see the way so plainly for others, I thought I was not a Christian, because I had not been sufficiently convicted. I would retire into the woods, and beg the Lord not to let me be deceived. I wished my burden back again, that I might watch more closely, and if the Lord would remove it, I would know more about it.. I also thought if I was truly converted, there would be more of a revolution in my whole man. And while I would be thus engaged, my mind would become sensibly attracted with the beauties and excellencies of the Saviour, and I could experience a joy unspeakable; but presently

* This feeling always attends conversion.

I would get into the same old distress, and conclude that *I could not be a Christian.* This lasted about four days before I could fully claim the promise. And even then I continued to doubt, frequently, my acceptance with God, seeing so much imperfection in every thing I did. But on the 10th day of June, 1802, I ventured to tell to the church what the Lord had done, as I hoped, for my soul, and I was received. On the next day I was baptized; and coming up out of the water, I had a strong desire to exhort the people, but the enemy of my soul suggested, 'You have gone too far already; for in a short time you will turn out as bad as ever'—and I yielded, and said nothing. But it was to me one of the most happy days of my life. I felt that I was honored inexpressibly to be permitted to follow my Saviour.* A sense of my own unworthiness was my only grief.

---

* This feeling is common to all baptized believers. —They have "the answer of a good conscience." 1 Pet. iii. 21. The Eunuch "went on his way rejoicing." Acts. viii. 39. R. F.

"I now had a severe struggle, for I found myself troubled with vain thoughts, and concluded, that if I was a Christian I certainly could get clear of them. I prayed and strove for some time against them, and still found these enemies haunting me, until it was impressed as strongly upon my mind as if it had been a human voice; *In yourself you are a poor helpless creature, and all your strength and sufficiency are in Christ.*" This gave me considerable relief. My mind was deeply impressed with the lost state of sinners, which impression extended to heathen nations, with such vehemence, that I frequently shed tears on the subject. A sense of my unworthiness kept me back until my mind became so earnestly drawn out, that one Lord's-day night at a camp-meeting at the church where my membership was, I exhorted and prayed for the first time publicly. From this period I went on, occasionally exhorting, and sometimes saying a few things on some passage of Scripture. But I labored almost constantly under awful doubts, as to my gracious state.

When I had appointments to preach, I
would frequently wish they had not been
made, such was my sense of my unworthiness. I would then think of exhorting
sinners, as I felt unfit to address Christians;
but as I would proceed in my exhortations,
I would become so filled with the love of
the Saviour, that I would get all on fire,
as it were, and would be telling the Christians how happy they would be in heaven.
One day I was deeply distressed with the
state of my heart, and was reading a book*
in which the author was treating on experi-
mental religion. He said, '*None but a
true believer mourns over a hard heart.*' I
knew I was mourning over *my* hard heart.
Tears flowed freely, and my doubts were
gone for a time; but they returned. I was
strongly tempted to disbelieve the reality of
religion, and even the existence of God; and
this temptation was so strong, that I was
afraid to breathe without prayer. My con-
stant prayer was, 'Lord have mercy on
me, and deliver *me* from this temptation.'

* What a blessing to have good books to read! R. F.

This continued some time. I was teaching a school, and one afternoon an awful thunder-storm arose, which frightened the children very greatly during its continuance. These words of the poet occurred to my mind—

> 'The God that rules on high,
>   And thunders when he please;
> That rides upon the stormy sky
>   And manages the seas;—
>
> This awful God is *mine*,
>   *My* father and *my* love,
> He will send down his heavenly powers,
>   To carry *me* above.'

" Here my doubts were removed, and an impression was left on my mind which has been beneficial ever since; and those awful temptations have never been permitted to return. Here, too, I may adopt the language of the hymn—' Blessed be the name of the Lord,'—

> 'Many days have passed since then,
>   Many changes I have seen;
> Yet have been upheld till now—
>   Who could hold me up but THOU?'

"I obtained license to preach in Union District, South Carolina, in 1803, and in 1804 removed to Buncombe county, North Carolina, on account of bad health. On the third day of August, I preached my first sermon there. I then went preaching about through 'the hill country,' inviting sinners to come to the Saviour;—telling them the way of salvation through the Redeemer.

"In 1805, I commenced preaching, in evenings, in a destitute settlement, near where I was teaching a school on Cane Creek. Brother James Whitaker and myself drew up Articles of Faith, as we could not find any in the country; and we collected all the members intending to be in the constitution, and examined them on the Articles. All being agreed, a presbytery was invited to attend. The presbytery was pleased with our Articles of Faith, and so the church was organized. Two of the members were, at the same time, ordained to the deacon's office, and I was ordained to the work of the ministry. At the next meeting, I baptized four professed believers, and the work of the Lord continued for a length of time. Some were received for baptism at almost every meeting."

Thus closes the account which Elder Posey gives of his conversion, and of his introduction into the work of the gospel ministry. Had he lived a few years longer, he no doubt would have completed his design, and the public would have been put in possession of a full account of his labors at Valley Towns, and among the Indians elsewhere. He would have given a general history of his abundant services after his removal from the Cherokee country.

CHAPTER III.

Revival of the Missionary Cause among Baptists in Europe—Among the Baptists in America.—American Board of Commissioners.—Triennial Convention.—Valley Town Mission among the Cherokee Indians.—Mr. Posey's agency and influence among them.

To be truly a Christian minister, is to be a Christian missionary; and he who has the spirit of Christ possesses the genuine missionary spirit. Whoever reads the Acts of the Apostles must perceive that the early disciples possessed this spirit in a large measure. The Acts of the Apostles may, with much propriety, be considered a Missionary Journal of the labors of the inspired heralds of salvation. When the blessed Jesus commissioned his apostles to "Go into all the world and preach the gospel to every creature," he fitted them for the work by imparting to them his own spirit, "*good will to men*"—*to all men*. Where this is wantng, no matter what else the individual may possess, the life—the soul of the commission is wanting, and the individual is not moved of the Holy Spirit to preach—IS NOT CALLED OF GOD TO THE WORK.

It is worthy of remark that whenever the Great Head of the Church is about to accomplish a peculiar purpose of mercy towards mankind, he invariably pours out a spirit of prayer and supplication upon his people; who, like the disciples on the day of Pentecost, present, "with one accord," their petitions before the throne of grace, and plead the promises on which their Divine and exalted Master had previously caused them to rest. This was literally the fact in respect to the churches and ministers of the Baptist denomination in England. It is worthy of record that the "CONCERT FOR PRAYER," one hour on the first Monday evening in every month, originated at a Baptist association, held at Nottingham, England, in 1784. The object of this concert-prayer meeting was declared to be, "*For the revival of genuine religion, and* *the extension of the Redeemer's kingdom throughout the earth."* In a short time thousands of the pious of all denominations, in England and America, united to present their prayers to him who has all power in heaven and in earth, for the accomplishment of this glorious result. Not only with the Baptists of England originated the monthly concert-prayer meeting, but with them originated the first regularly organized purely evangelical Foreign Missionary Society in that country.* In answer to the prayers of the friends of Jesus Christ, God brought forward that remarkable man, Rev. William Carey, from obscurity, full of the Holy Ghost and wisdom, and sent him out to British India, where he planted the standard of Gospel truth. His motto was

"Expect great things from God;—
Attempt great things for God."

In America, we soon after notice a similar movement in the cause of Christ. The

* See Choules' History of Missions, and the History of the English Baptist Missionary Society.

souls of some pious young men at college, preparing "for the work of the ministry," were warmed up with the spirit of Christ—the spirit of missions. They began to wrestle with God in prayer, and seek direction in the great work whereunto they felt he had called them.

"It is difficult," says Dr. Choules in his History of Missions, to "obtain a minute account of the original foundation and agents of the Missions from America. With that denominational feeling which is common, the Baptists and the Congregationalists, each claim for their own missionaries, the honor of the first movement, in the attempt to evangelise a portion of the world through the American churches. The Baptists assign the laurel to Adoniram Judson, while the Congregationalists claim it for Samuel John Mills. Upon such a subject, where such noble spirits are the actors, it would be wrong to contend. Indeed, such respect have we for the piety, the benevolence and zeal, both of Judson and Mills, that we esteem it a matter of but little importance, to say which of the two was the honored instrument of God in commencing so glorious a work."

As Elder Posey was almost all his life in the work of the ministry, and intimately connected with the great work of Missions to the Cherokee Indians, we have thought proper to call the reader's attention to a brief sketch of the origin of missions in these United States. And in order to do this it may not be amiss to insert, in this place, an extract from a letter from the pen of Mr. Judson himself,* written to Elder Luther Rice. He says—

"*My Dear Brother Rice:*

"You ask me to give you some account of my first missionary impressions, and then of my early associates. Mine were occasioned by reading Buchanan's 'Star in the East,' in the year 1809, at Andover Theological Seminary. Though I do not now consider that sermon as peculiarly excellent, it produced a powerful effect on my mind.

* See Rice's Memoir, page 81.

For some days, I was unable to attend to the studies of my class, and spent my time in wondering at my past stupidity, depicting the most romantic scenes in missionary life, and roving about the college rooms, declaiming on the subject of missions. My views were very incorrect, and my feelings extravagant; but yet I have always felt thankful to God for bringing me into a state of excitement, which was, perhaps, necessary, in the first instance, to enable me to break the strong attachments I felt to home and country, and to endure the thought of abandoning all my wonted pursuits and animating prospects. That excitement soon passed away, but it left a strong desire to prosecute my inquiries, and to ascertain the path of duty.

"It was during a solitary walk in the woods, behind the college, while meditating and praying on the subject, and feeling half inclined to give it up, that the command of Christ, "Go into all the world and preach the gospel to every creature," was presented to my mind with such clearness and power, that I came to a full decision; and though great difficulties appeared in my way, resolved to obey the command at all events. But at that period, no provision had been made in America, for a foreign mission; and for several months after reading Buchanan, I found none among the students who viewed the subject as I did, and no minister in the place or neighborhood, who gave me any encouragement; and I thought I should be under the necessity of going to England, and placing myself under foreign patronage.

"My earliest missionary associate was Nott, who, though he had recently entered the Seminary, (in the early part of 1810,) was a member of the same class with myself. He had considered the subject for several months, but had not fully made up his mind. About the same time Mills, Richards and others joined the seminary from Williams' College, where they had, for some time, been in the habit of meeting for prayer and conversation on the subject of missions; but they entered the junior class, and had several years of theological study before them. Newell was the next accession from my own class. As for Hall, he was preaching at Woodbury, Connecticut. I heard that he once thought favorably of missions, and I wrote him a short letter. He had just received a call to settle in that place, and was deliberating whether it was his duty to accept it or not, when the letter was put into his hand. He instantly came to a decision; and the next rising sun saw him on his way to Andover. I think he arrived about the time of the meeting of the General Association of Ministers at Bradford, in the summer of 1810. I do not, however, recollect him present at that meeting, nor was his name attached to the paper which was presented to the association, and which was originally signed by Nott, Newell, Mills, Rice, Richards and myself; though at the suggestion of Dr. Spring, your name and Richards', (which happened to be last,) were struck off, for fear of alarming the association with too large a number.

"I have thought that the providence of

God was conspicuously manifested in bringing us all together from different and distant parts. Some of us had been considering the subject of missions a long time, and some but recently. Some, and indeed the greater part, had thought chiefly of domestic missions, and efforts among the neighboring tribes of Indians, without contemplating the abandonment of country, and devotement for life. How evident it is, that the Spirit of God had been operating in different places, upon different individuals, preparing the way for those movements which have since pervaded the American churches, and will continue to increase until the kingdoms of this world become the kingdom of our Lord and his anointed."

In referring to this interesting era in the history of the missionary enterprise, by the American churches, it will be justifiable on the part of the writer, as it will be profitable to the reader, to introduce a quotation from a letter of Elder Luther Rice to a friend. He says:—

"After the society at Andover was well

established, the views of the brethren were turned very much towards the East. Judson was the first, as far as I know, who mentioned Burmah. He had read Buchanan's 'Star in the East,' his 'Christian Researches in Asia,' and ' Captain Simon's Embassy to Ava.' He insisted that the East afforded much the widest and most promising field for missionary exertions, and that the path of duty led him in that direction.

"In June, 1810, Gordon Hall, who had been preaching some time, and who had been invited to become the pastor of a church in Connecticut, came to Andover to consult with the professors whether he ought not to hold himself devoted to missionary labor among the heathen. (O! how I love to trace important events to minute incidents!) It happened to be but a day or two before the meeting of the General Association of all the evangelical part of the ministers of Massachusetts, at Bradford, where the parents of Ann Hasseltine lived, ten miles from the institution, in Andover.

"The coming, and the object of the coming of Hall, so enlivened the missionary sentiments and feelings, particularly in the bosoms of the members of the Society, that Judson immediately wrote the memorial,*

* The following is the Memorial alluded to, in Mrs. Ann H. Judson's Life, page 39. See also Choules' History of Missions, vol. ii. page 236.

"The undersigned, members of the Divinity College, respectfully request the attention of their reverend fathers, convened in the General Association at Bradford, to the following statement and inquiries.

They beg leave to state, that their minds have been long impressed with the duty and importance of personally attempting a mission to the heathen; that the impressions on their minds have induced a serious, and, they trust, a prayerful consideration of the subject in its various attitudes, particularly in relation to the probable success and the difficulties attending such an attempt; and that after examining all the information which they can obtain, they consider themselves as devoted to this work for life, whenever God, in his providence, shall open the way.

They now offer the following inquiries, on which they solicit the opinion and advice of the Association; whether with their present views and feelings they ought to renounce the object of missions as visionary or impracticable; if not, whether they ought to direct their attention to the Eastern or the Western world; whether they may expect patronage and support from which you see in the Memoirs of Mrs. Ann H. Judson, addressed to that body of ministers." (See Rice's Memoir, page 86.)

a missionary society in this country, or must commit themselves to the direction of a European society, and what preparatory measures they ought to take, previous to actual engagement.

The undersigned, feeling their youth and inexperience, look up to their fathers in the church, and respectfully solicit their advice, direction and prayers.

ADONIRAM JUDSON, JR.,
SAMUEL NOTT, JR.,
SAMUEL J. MILLS,
SAMUEL NEWELL,
JAMES RICHARDS,
LUTHER RICE."

It will be remembered that when Judson drew up the above memorial, it was signed as above; but before it was laid before the Association at Bradford, it was deemed prudent to strike off the two last names, lest so great a number would embarrass their operations, and defeat the cherished object of their desires. —The reader may feel anxious to know what has been the destiny—the end of those master-spirits in the great work of evangelizing the heathen. Men whose souls, like Humphrey Posey's, burned with holy enthusiasm, for the salvation of their benighted fellow-men.

JUDSON.—First on the Memorial, was the last on

The above association of Congregationalists appointed a committee, to whom the memorial was referred. The committee re-

the mission field. He died fifteen minutes past four o'clock in the afternoon of May the 12th, 1850, on board the French barque Aristide Marie, bound for the Isle of Bourbon. At 8 o'clock in the afternoon of the same day he was committed to the deep in latitude 13 degrees North, longitude 93 East. He lived to translate the Bible into the Burman language, and had nearly finished a great Dictionary of the Burman language. He was in Burmah near 37 years.

MILLS.—Died June 16, 1818.—Buried in the Atlantic Ocean, on his way to England from a mission to Africa.

NEWELL.—Died of cholera at Bombay, India, May 30, 1821.

RICHARDS.—Died August 3, 1822, in Ceylon.

RICE.—Died in Edgefield District, South Carolina, Sept. 25, 1836.

NOTT.—After his arrival at Calcutta, his health became poor, and it was deemed advisable for him to return to America. He is the pastor of the Congregational church, in Wareham, Massachusetts. When Dr. Judson visited America, Nott, hearing of his arrival, set out for Boston with all speed to greet him. It was in Bowdoin Square church, while they were singing, he passed rapidly up the aisle into the pulpit, and embraced Dr. J. with uncommon warmth and ardor—which was as ardently reciprocated. Mr. Nott is probably still at Wareham. R. F.

ported favorably, and consequently nine commissioners were appointed by the same body. They formed in September, 1810, the constitution of the *"American Board of Commissioners for Foreign Missions,"* which now embraces the entire Congregational and Presbyterian denominations.

"From this arose," continues Elder Rice, in his letter, "*the Baptist General Convention*, formed in May, 1814, and since more or less distinctly out of the same range of evangelical influence, the American Bible Society, the American Tract Society, the Baptist General Tract Society, [now the American Baptist Publication Society,] the Columbian College, the Newton Theological Institution, and I know not how many other things of more or less importance. Glory be to God."

After the formation of the American Board of Commissioners for Foreign Missions, Mr. Judson and his associates expected and desired an immediate appointment as missionaries. But the Board being as yet unprovided with funds, Mr. Judson solicited and obtained leave of the Board to visit England, to ascertain whether any measures of co-operation could be concerted between the London Missionary Society and the American Board, and whether any assistance could be obtained from that Society in case the Board should be unable to sustain a mission. He sailed in January, 1811, for England. But no concert of measures could be arranged. The London Society agreed to support Mr. Judson and his companions as missionaries, *if the American Board should not be able to do it.* He returned to America, and the Board resolved to sustain a mission to Burmah, and Judson, Nott, Newell and Hall, were immediately appointed. Mr. Rice was appointed afterwards. On the 6th of February, 1812, they were ordained in the Tabernacle church in Salem, Massachusetts, On the 18th of June, 1812, they landed in Calcutta, where they were met and welcomed to India, by the venerable Dr. Carey, Baptist Missionary from England. Mr. and Mrs. Judson remained in Calcutta two months, during which time Mr. Judson and his wife, and also Mr. Rice, who had now arrived in India, became convinced that their sentiments on baptism were unsupported by the Word of God, and they became Baptists. Mr. Judson's doubts commenced while engaged in translating the New Testament, on his passage from America, and he frequently said during the voyage, that the Baptists were right in their views on the subject. On the first Lord's-day in September, 1812, he and his wife were baptized by Dr. Carey; and on the first day of November following, Luther Rice was baptized by Mr. Ward. This change of sentiment on the part of these distinguished movers of the great mission cause among the Congregationalists necessarily produced their separation from the patronage and support of the American Board, and of course they had now to look for support in some other quarter. Mr. Judson therefore addressed a letter to Dr. Bolles, Baptist minister, of Salem, in which he says: "Under these circumstances I look to you.

Alone, in this foreign heathen land, I make my appeal to those, whom, with their permission, I will call *my Baptist brethren in the United States.*"

It was now decidedly the opinion of Judson and Rice, that they must rely on the Baptist denomination in America for support. Rice, therefore, returned to the land of his birth to stir up the Baptists to the work of the Lord in the support of foreign missions. It was on the 7th of September, 1813, he arrived at New York. But as the Board of Commissioners was to meet in Boston on the 15th, he hastened on to discharge what he considered his obligations to the Board. The Board treated him and his communications, in reference to his becoming a Baptist, very coolly. They voted that they considered the relation between him and the Board dissolved, from the date of his letter from Calcutta, announcing the fact of his change of sentiment.

In consulting with the Baptist brethren in Boston, it was thought necessary to proceed, at once, to the adoption of measures which might excite the Baptists of this country to combine their energies in the mission cause. They concluded to call a meeting of delegates from different parts of the country, as soon as practicable, to embody the energies of the denomination, for the purpose of conducting these operations on an enlarged scale. In September, 1813, Rice set out from Boston on a tour towards the South, in order to accomplish the designs above stated. He visited New York, Philadelphia, Washington, Richmond, Charleston, and Savannah, and many parts of Georgia, Carolina, and Virginia, laying before the brethren, wherever he went, the objects of his mission; and he found them ready to co-operate with him. Delegates met in Philadelphia on the 18th of May, 1814, from different parts of the United States, and after a careful consideration of the whole subject, for several days, they decided, unanimously, to form a "*General Convention of the Baptist denomination in the United States for Foreign Missions.*"

This was afterwards denominated *the Triennial Convention,* and has generally been spoken of in this way.

Thus we have given a brief account of the origin of those great missionary combinations which have been in very successful operation in England and America for a number of years. We have seen that the Baptists have had great agency in awakening up and putting in motion the slumbering energies of the people of God on both continents. We have seen with what zeal that distinguished servant of the Lord, Dr. William Carey, was fired amongst his kindred spirits in Great Britain. And we have witnessed the rise and the growing interest of missions in this glorious land of civil and religious liberty.

The names of Judson, Rice, and others, who labored with them, will long be cherished in the recollection of American churches. Though they now rest from their labors, their works do follow them. And though the mortal remains of Rice sleep quietly in the dust at "*Pine Pleasant*

Church," in Edgefield, South Carolina—and though Adoniram Judson has gone down beneath the dark wave of the Indian Ocean, to await the period when "the sea shall give up her dead," yet they are not forgotten—they shall be " in everlasting remembrance."

But we must return from this apparent digression. The reader will probably ask, *What has this sketch of the rise and progress of modern missions to do with the history of Humphrey Posey?* Let it be remembered, in answer to this question, that while the God of missions was raising up men to go far hence to the gentiles,—to the benighted nations of the Eastern continent,—he was moving the spirit of this obscure man, in the " hill country" of North Carolina, to proclaim the way of salvation to the Cherokee Indians. While Rice and others, (pious young men preparing for the ministry,) were students at Williams College, and were deeply impressed with a sense of the perishing condition of the heathen nations, and while they were pouring out their prayers to God for direction, Posey was in the work of the ministry in Buncombe county, preaching at night, and teaching school in the day. While those young men of Williams' College were retiring for prayer on Saturdays, to their consecrated spot, by the side of a large haystack, in a field on the banks of the river Hoosac, in the fall of 1807, Posey was lifting up his voice like a trumpet among the mountains. He was in Christ, and in the ministry, before they were, and before the organization of the "American Board of Commissioners for Foreign Missions," and consequently before the formation of the General Convention of the Baptist denomination in the United States for foreign missions.

Posey was licensed to preach in 1803, and ordained in 1806, as has already been stated. The organization of the Baptist Convention was accomplished mainly through the instrumentality of Luther Rice, who, in his tour through the Southern States, in 1813, had formed some acquaintance with Elder Posey, either personally or from report. The Convention, after having made some provision for the support of missions in foreign lands, was now desirous to send the gospel to the aborigines of our own country. In the winter of 1817, Elder Luther Rice, (then agent of the Baptist Board of Foreign Missions, of the Triennial Convention,) wrote to Elder Posey, requesting information in reference to the practicability of establishing a mission among the Cherokee Indians, residing mostly in the western part of North Carolina, and the northern portion of the State of Georgia. Posey's heart was in the work, and had been for some time burning with anxiety to preach the gospel to his neighbors, the untutored Cherokees. Having lived in their vicinity, he was well prepared to give the desired information. He wrote to Elder Rice, and the letter was laid before the Board at Philadelphia, and Dr. William Staughton, the Corresponding Secretary, was requested to address Elder Posey, in order to ascertain whether his services could be obtained as their missionary. Several letters passed between them. The following may be interesting to the reader, as well as to the friends of both of these excellent ministers of Jesus Christ. Dr. Staughton to Elder Posey, writes as follows:

"*Philadelphia, Oct.* 16, 1817.
MY DEAR BROTHER,—

At a meeting of the Baptist Board of Foreign Missions, on Monday last, your favor of August the 26th was submitted and considered. The Board, anxious to see "the light of life" spreading among the Cherokees, and on the western frontiers generally, and pleased to find your heart set upon the good work, enter with pleasure into your feelings and views. They wish you to accept immediately an appointment, as their missionary for twelve months. The more immediate sphere of action they must leave to your judgment, only remarking in general, that the frontier of the country, and the Indians, they wish you more immediately to keep in view. What you can do in relation to schools, &c., with the Divine blessing, you must inform us. With respect to compensation, the Board could have wished you had been a little more explicit. They submit to you the sum of $500 for twelve months. This is their idea at the commencement. They wish to be frugal, but they feel it their duty to make their missionaries comfortable. You can draw for the above sum as you may find it convenient. May the Lord be with you and bless you.

Very affectionately your brother,
WM. STAUGHTON, Cor. Sec."

The following is Elder Posey's answer to the above, accepting the appointment:

"*Asheville, N. C., Nov.* 24, 1817.
REV. AND DEAR BROTHER,—

I wrote to you by the last mail, but on receiving yours of the 16th October, I felt it my duty to send you an immediate answer. I wish to communicate to the Board, that with gratitude I accept the appointment of missionary to the Cherokees, humbly requesting that the Board will bear me up in their prayers, and beseech the blessed Jesus to ask for the poor benighted Cherokees, as a part of his immediate inheritance.

As it respects my compensation, suffice it to say, I am fully satisfied with the decision of the Board on the subject. I shall endeavor to begin about the 1st of December, shall keep a regular record of my proceedings, and communicate the same quarterly, or oftener.

The confidence placed in me by the Board, while it makes me feel unworthy, still binds them to me in a manner not easily to be expressed, and I hope never to be forgotten. May Heaven smile upon you, my dear brother, and may the happy period speedily roll round, when the earth shall be full of the knowledge of the Lord, and his high praises be sounded in every place.

Yours, in the blessed Jesus,
H. POSEY."

Thus a wide and effectual door is opened, and the long-cherished desire of his heart is granted, THAT HE MIGHT PREACH THE GOSPEL TO THE INDIANS.

After receiving his appointment, he commenced, on the 1st of December, 1817, a tour of preaching among the Indians, and the white people on the frontier. In 1818 and 1819, he formed a very extensive acquaintance with the tribe. He visited Charles Hicks, one of the principal chiefs, and a true friend to Indian reform, " and I trust," says Posey, "*a real Christian.*"

At a grand council of the chiefs at New Town, Oct. 27, 1819, he obtained their hearty consent, and promise of co-operation to establish a school amongst them at Valley Town. Having now determined on a location for a mission school, under the patronage of the Baptists, it was necessary, by stipulations entered into by the chiefs, that the consent and aid of the President of the United States should be secured. Consequently Posey, with that promptitude and decision of character for which he was so remarkable, proceeded at an early date in 1820, to Washington City. While there, he formed an acquaintance with a number of the distinguished men of the nation. The Hon. J. C. Calhoun, then Secretary of War, promised, in behalf of the government, to defray half of the expense of the school buildings when finished; and further aid when the school should be in actual operation, allowing the Baptist schools in the Cherokee nation an equal share of the money appropriated for schools in that tribe.

It may be proper to state here, that this, though the first school established among the Cherokees by the Baptists, was not the first in the Cherokee nation. In 1817, Posey commenced his missionary labors in the nation; and in the fall of that year the American Board of Commissioners established a school at a place they called Brainerd. This school had secured an appropriation from the government of the United States, and when Posey visited Washington City, as we have seen, he obtained from the government the promise of an equal share with that of other denominations. It may also be stated, that although the "American Board of Commissioners" was organized four years earlier than the "Baptist Triennial Convention," yet they were not a year earlier in sending a missionary among the Cherokees, and they were not a year before the Baptists in the establishment of a school. Years before this Elder Posey would have gone into the nation, "once and again," but he "lacked opportunity." Now the Baptist Board afforded him ample means to allow him fully to develop the desires of his heart.

From Washington City he proceeded to Philadelphia, where he was cordially received by the churches. These were the days of Staughton, McLaughlin, Jones, and others of contemporary and congenial spirits. On his way thither, he preached in many of the churches, and formed valuable acquaintance with many of the most eminent ministers in the denomination. In his

Journal of travel, he mentions the names of many ministers with whom he had pleasant and profitable interviews. At Middleborough, in Virginia, he became acquainted with Rev. J. L. Dagg, now President of Mercer University, Georgia. While at Washington City, he was cordially entertained by the friends of the Redeemer, and records in his Journal, as a matter of thanksgiving to God, the general success which seemed to attend the object of his agency. Though brought up among the mountains, and of course not accustomed to city etiquette —*city ways*—he possessed the happy faculty of being easy in his intercourse with his brethren under almost any circumstances.

The writer of these pages remembers a very pleasing incident which Mr. Posey told him occurred during one of his visits to Philadelphia, when he was preaching in the church of the late Elder James McLaughlin. It is not an unusual thing, in many of the churches in our back-woods, for the preacher to close a meeting by singing, and going round through the congregation, the mean while, shaking hands with the brethren and people generally. To this custom Elder Posey had often been a witness in the regions in which he had labored as a minister, and he was himself not unfriendly to it, but would often engage in it. Feeling that the usages of the good people in and about Philadelphia, were not like those of the people in the country where he had been accustomed to preach, he remarked to brother McLaughlin, that if he should become a little excited, and should do such a thing among his people, he hoped he would not take any offence at it. Elder McLaughlin told him to use his liberty among his people, assuring him he should not be offended at it, and he did not think his people would. Posey, it seems, had preached several times to this people, and had become much attached to them. He began to feel at home. When preaching to them on one occasion, he became unusually warm while speaking of the love of Jesus to lost sinners, and while urging upon Christians the duty of making efforts to have the gospel preached to every creature. In the warmth of his heart, he exclaimed in the language of Jehu to Jehonadab, "Is thine heart right, as my heart is with thy heart? If it be, give me thy hand." And in uttering these words, he immediately gave brother McLaughlin his hand, started from the pulpit, and went through the congregation, giving them his hand, and speaking all the while, of the love of the adorable Saviour. He stated, that his precious brother McLaughlin, for that was an epithet he frequently used, in speaking of brethren whom he very specially loved, seemed not offended, but rather delighted with the apparent heart-felt piety and godly simplicity which prevailed in the church and congregation.

From Philadelphia he came home, as he went, not in coaches or stages, but on horseback, preaching. His Journal is filled with appointments and notes in reference to his success, all going to show him as a laborious, business-doing man.

In 1821, he again visited Philadelphia, to consult with the Board, and to procure supplies for the Valley Town school. He preached in nearly all the churches in the city, and obtained the promise of the Board to furnish a mission family to unite with him in the labors of the school. He continued his valuable and highly acceptable services until the year 1824. The promised assistance arrived in 1821, consisting of Rev. Thomas Roberts and his wife, Rev. Evan Jones and his wife, Isaac Cleaver, a blacksmith, and John Farrier, a farmer. These, with their families, together with Miss Jones, Miss Cleaver, and Miss Lewis, sailed from Philadelphia, in 1821, laden with clothing for their schools, and other things necessary for a large missionary establishment. Elder Roberts and Mr. Farrier discontinued their labors in 1824, and Mr. Cleaver continued until the close of the next year. Elder Evan Jones continued until the Indians removed to the Territory, assigned to them by the government, beyond the Mississippi.

Purity and innocence furnish no security against the tongue of the calumniator. As might be expected, the "wickedness of the wicked" sought to blacken the reputation of this indefatigable missionary. Satan's kingdom, through the omnipotence of the Divine truths which he proclaimed, was receiving a death-blow in that quarter. The success which attended his labors amongst the Cherokees, and the white population on the frontiers, was such as to wake up the morbid energies of worldly-minded, whiskey-loving professors, and to excite the bitter gall of the haters of gospel light. Hence, the hue and cry against the mission school, and against the waste of money and means, was heard at Valley Town. The whole was declared to be a matter of speculation, and a money-making business to those entrusted with its management. Some good men, it is feared, had a hand in this foul work. That there would be much expense incurred in the erection of the necessary buildings, it is easy to conceive. The place was remote from the white population, and far distant from any market. Ill-disposed persons, and there are always too many such, who know not the value of such work, are ever ready to clamor. To put to silence all such, the French Broad Association, at the request of Elder Posey, appointed a committee, consisting of Elder Jeremiah Taylor, William Kimsey, Garrett Dewees, and Adam Carn, to visit the missionary establishment, and report at the next session. Only Dewees and Carn met. They report:—

"*That they had done as they were requested, and found the school in a very flourishing condition, fully up to their highest expectations. That notwithstanding there have been large sums of money expended for the establishment, yet not unnecessarily; and that they, therefore, do heartily recommend its promotion.*"

The venerable Deacon, James Whitaker, in a letter, says, "I was at Valley Town in 1821, six or eight weeks, and during that time, I had full opportunity to know every thing in and about the establishment;

and, I can say, a more attentive and faithful man could not be found, and the Cherokees universally esteem him as a good man. At the mention of his name, those who still remain in the country,* will brighten up with a smile on their countenance."

In 1836, this school is reported in I. M. Allen's Register, as being in a flourishing condition, "*And to this day the Cherokees have more confidence in Humphrey Posey than they have in any other man living.*"— Page 166.

In reference to this missionary station, Rev. Mr. Jones states, that it contained in 1833, *one hundred and eighty-five members;* and at another church, formed seventy-five miles west of Valley Town, there were seventy-three members, gathered principally by the labors of Jesse Bushyhead, a Cherokee convert.

* A few Indians did remain after the body of the nation had gone to the Indian Territory.

CHAPTER IV.

Character of Elder Posey as a Christian.—A preacher.—A pastor.—A yoke-fellow in the ministry.—Letter from Elder A. Webb.—Interesting anecdote.—Dr. Howell's letter.—Respect of the Indians for him.

THE developments of vital godliness in the lives of many of those who profess religion, are not always such as to leave it unquestionable that they are the children of grace. God requires, and the world expects, that His people should make full proof of their claims to discipleship. He who has the profession without the principle, or the place without the piety, of a true Christian, is as the "sounding brass," or the "tinkling cymbal." He may boast of his faith, his zeal, his knowledge, his unbounded benevolence, but he is nothing,—God has said it.

The individual who claims to be a son of God, on the ground that he remembers the time, the place, and the circumstances of his conversion, while he exhibits none of that meek, lowly, and forgiving temper which characterized the meek and lowly Saviour, is deceived; "*that man's religion is vain.*" Elder Posey has given us, it is true, in his own words, an account of the time, the place, and the circumstances of his conversion; but his spirit, his conversation was "as becometh the gospel of Christ," and afforded the highest evidence of his having "passed from death unto life." Heart-felt piety, not that talkative kind of religion, which is found in words and not in deeds, marked the whole course of his life. He was "a lover of good men," and all good men who knew him loved him in return.

As a Minister of the Gospel, he was laborious in the discharge of the duties of his high calling, and prompt in attending his appointments to preach. His sermons were sensible and interesting expositions of the Sacred Scriptures. Doctrinally and practically, he was what may be termed a sound-headed, warm-hearted preacher. His sermons were not a boisterous vociferation of Bible truth, disconnected and inappropriate; but they were generally plain, calm, thoughtful, and well adapted to the spiritual wants of his audience. He studied the Bible well, and preached well what it taught. His library was well selected, for a mere English scholar. He had Gill's Exposition of the Bible, Gill's Body of Divinity, abridged by Dr. Staughton, Fuller's Works, Newton's Works, and several commentaries, besides miscellaneous works, of great value to the Bible student. He read them and profited by them. He was not in the habit of attempting to show off as a man of reading; nor did he feel inclined to indulge in strained, far-fetched and absurd theories— he was not " a novice."

As a Pastor, few men ever succeeded better in securing the kind attention and hearty co-operation of their people, than did Elder Posey. To this circumstance, no doubt, in a very great degree, is owing very much of the success which attended his labors in his Churches; for no Preacher or Pastor, can do much in building up a Church, and carrying forward the interests of the Kingdom of Jesus Christ on earth, without the aid of those with whom he is connected in this great work. The blessed Son of God prayed that all who should believe on him through the word of his Apostles might "BE ONE, THAT THE WORLD MIGHT BELIEVE" that he was the promised Saviour. What a mischievous thing among the people of God, is division and contention! Hence the Apostle Paul, earnestly and repeatedly rebuked those in his day who were sowing contention among Brethren. He says in his Epistle to the Romans, "We being many are one body in Christ, and every one members one of another." Rom. xii. 6. In his Epistle to the Corinthians, "that there should be no schism in the body, but that the members should have the same care one for another." 1 Cor. xii. 25. Who can contemplate the beauty and the importance of that passage in the Epistle to the Colossians without being at once convinced that divisions among

Christians are a sore evil. "Let the peace of God rule in your hearts, to the which ye are also called in one body." Col. iii. 15. O, how tender! how deep the solicitude of the Apostle in reference to this subject! Hear him again, in the overflowing of a soul full of that fervor of spirit which became the highly exalted position which he occupied. *Now I beseech you, brethren, by the name of our Lord Jesus Christ, that ye all speak the same thing, and that there be no divisions among you, but that ye be perfectly joined together in the same mind and in the same judgment.* 1 Cor. i. 10.

Possessing, in a large degree, that love for the peace and the prosperity of the spiritual Jerusalem, which always characterizes the "good minister of Jesus Christ," and having much of that wisdom which is profitable to direct in the use of the means to be employed for the accomplishment of this object, so dear to his heart, Elder Posey was rarely found on the wrong side in cases of difficulty. He was a good judge of human character, and rarely failed to place a correct estimate on the words or the works of men. High-minded, open-hearted, candid and firm in his bearing, he held out few inducements to the under-handed, designing sycophant to lean upon him in order to give importance to himself, or to accomplish some selfish end on his own behalf. The determination of the Psalmist, David, when he entered on the discharge of the duties of King in Israel, is that which regulated the conduct of Elder Posey in the exercise of the duties of a Pastor. "I will set no wicked thing before mine eyes; I hate the work of them that turn aside; it shall not cleave to me. A froward heart shall depart from me; I will not know a wicked person. Whoso privily slandereth his neighbor, him will I cut off; him that hath a high look and a proud heart will not I suffer. Mine eyes shall be upon the faithful of the land, that they may dwell with me; he that walketh in a perfect way, he shall serve me. He that worketh deceit, shall not dwell within my house; he that telleth lies shall not tarry in my sight. I will early destroy all the wicked of the land, that I may cut off all wicked doers from the city of the Lord." Ps. ci.

To instruct the people of his charge, and to elevate the standard of personal piety amongst them, was a leading feature in his ministrations. Hence all circus-going, backgammon playing, and the like, were sure to meet an appropriate reproof, when any of his brethren should be found guilty of such inconsistencies. Pope, in one of his letters, asserts that "To attack vices in the abstract, without touching persons, may be safe fighting indeed, but it is fighting with shadows." Elder Posey was pretty much of the same opinion, and consequently he did not conduct his spiritual warfare in that way. Paul, a greater than Pope, did not fail to specify, "Be not deceived; neither fornicators, nor idolaters, nor adulterers, nor effeminate, nor abusers of themselves with mankind, nor thieves, nor covetous, nor drunkards, nor revilers, nor extortioners, shall inherit the Kingdom of God. *And such were some of* YOU"—YOU CORINTHIANS. 1 Cor. vi. 9–11.

Elder Posey viewed the frequent changes in the pastoral relation with the churches as injurious in their general tendency, and was decidedly opposed to the custom, in many of the churches, of calling a Preacher annually. The connection existing between the Pastor and his flock, he considered as one of very peculiar character, and the feelings between him and them should always be of the kindest and most endearing character, and should not be broken off for trivial causes. He always sought to heal the little heart-burnings which might arise, either among the members of the churches of his *own charge*, or those which might spring up among the members of other churches towards *their Pastor*. He abhorred in a minister of Jesus Christ that unholy kind of feeling which sought to undermine or supplant a brother in the pastoral charge. He, therefore, had no ear to listen to complaints against the preacher in charge, nor would he seize upon these things, as affording himself an opportunity to work his way into a more desirable Pastorate.

AS A TRUE YOKE-FELLOW, his bearing towards his fellow-laborers in the work of the ministry, was dignified and Christian like. Courtesy he esteemed as a virtue among his brethren, which should always be observed in order to preserve the unity of the Spirit in the bonds of peace. He ever sought to build up, and never to pull down, the reputation of those who minister in holy things, knowing full well that whatever would seriously affect a minister's influence among his brethren, would injure his usefulness among others, and would be like loosening the strong pillars under an important edifice. He knew the import of that expression of the Apostle, "For now we live, if ye stand fast in the Lord."

Elder Alfred Webb, favorably known as a good minister of Jesus Christ, in the upper part of Georgia, and whose acquaintance with Elder Posey was long and intimate, has furnished in a letter, quite an interesting sketch of his life, from which only a few extracts can here be made. He writes:—

"My first acquaintance with Elder Humphrey Posey was in 1809 or 1810, when I was nine or ten years old, at my father's in Rutherford county, North Carolina. He was then living in Buncombe county, and attended several churches in adjacent parts. God blessed his labors in the above counties to the conversion of many sinners. He was engaged in school teaching, and many of his scholars, and numbers of citizens, will no doubt rejoice through eternity that Humphrey Posey ever visited Rutherford county. Some time after, he removed to Haywood county, where he was exceedingly useful in the hand of the Lord, in building up the churches in that part of the world.

"He left Haywood to take charge of a mission in the Cherokee nation, where he originated and attended the management of a very flourishing school, and preached over the nation by means of an interpreter, for the space of about five years. Eternity will unfold the good which this faithful servant of the Most High God effected in the moral condition of these rude people.

"No man probably ever possessed a more

un-ullied character, both as a citizen and a Minister of the Gospel; and though Mr. Posey did not possess a classical education, yet by his energetic and devoted efforts, he rendered himself famous in the Church of Christ. In sentiment he was a Calvinist, and possessed, in a high degree, a talent to explain the doctrine of election and predestination in a practical manner, so that the Free-will Baptists and the Arminians generally received him with love and admiration."

An anecdote furnished in the letter from which the above extract is made, may be properly introduced at this place. It shows the wit and the power which Elder Posey possessed in wielding the sword of the Spirit, the word of the Lord. The writer says:—

"Mr. Posey and myself being at Tuckasiege Association on the 20th of August, 1832, left to go to the French Broad Association, which was to convene on Saturday the 25th; and having appointment to preach on the route, on Friday I preached for him at Cany Creek, in Yancy county, he being sick. After the meeting we called at a gentleman's house to dine, in company with Elder Stephen Morgan. The gentleman's brother and wife called also, both being Freewill Baptists. After some conversation, he remarked to Brother Posey, 'My wife and myself feel very much disappointed in not hearing you preach to-day, after coming twelve miles for that purpose.' Mr. Posey remarked that they had heard the Gospel preached. But he still persisted that he was disappointed, inasmuch as he was the preacher he had come to hear. 'Well, said Posey, you believe what the brother preached to-day.' He answered he did. 'Well,' replied Posey, 'I could not have preached any thing else, to have kept within the covers of the Bible.' But the Free-willer appeared to be dissatisfied still. Elder Posey assumed a grave appearance, and said to him, 'Suppose I had occupied the pulpit to-day and said, 'Moreover, whom he did predestinate, them he also called; and whom he called, them he also justified; and whom he justified, them he also glorified; would you have believed me?' The Free-willer replied promptly, 'No, I would not.' 'No! said Posey; but thank God it is his precious word, and the gates of hell cannot prevail against it.' The Free-willer blushed in confusion."

This objector to the doctrine of election and predestination, it is feared, is a fair sample of hundreds and thousands. He was so unacquainted with his Bible, that he did not know what God had said by his holy apostle on this subject. Many are so ignorant of the language of the scriptures, that they do not know when the minister quotes from the sacred page; hence they object to these sublime and glorious doctrines, not knowing what they do. "They do err, not knowing the scriptures." Numbers, just like the above objector, will not believe what the preacher says, though, like Posey, he should exhibit the doctrine in the language of holy writ. Frequently, too, those professors of the religion of Christ, who know the least of the holy oracles, are the most confident, dogmatic, and obstinate in the defence of their peculiar notions on the subject of religion. It was unsafe for the cause of such to come in contact with Humphrey Posey.

A short letter from Dr. Howell will show, to some considerable extent, the place Elder Posey occupied in the estimation of our learned and talented ministers, at an early day, and also the place assigned him in his old age. The letter is here inserted entire, because of its brevity and appropriateness.

"*Nashville, Feb.* 12, 1849.
DEAR BROTHER FLEMING,—

I am not able to give you the information you desire, regarding our lamented brother Posey. When a boy, at my father's plantations, on the Neuse, I felt interested in the accounts that reached me, of his preaching in the upper part of the State. North Carolina has, very naturally, as my native place, always been dear to me. Upon its leading ministers, Mr. Posey amongst them, I always kept my eye, and with, if possible, a warmer interest after I left the State to reside, first in Virginia, and subsequently in Tennessee, than before. Nor did I cease to mark his course when he removed farther South. Rev. J. Wiseman, of this State, a man of eminent talents and usefulness, has often spoken to me of Mr. Posey as the pastor of his youth, and the minister by whom he was baptized. My information is of too general and limited a character to be of special service to you in your proposed Memoir. I saw our venerable brother once only, at Murfreesborough, in this State, some five years ago, when we were together for two days. I ever regarded him as a good minister of Jesus Christ, devoted in his piety, and useful in his labors.

Yours, truly,
R. B. C. HOWELL."

The expression, "devoted in his piety," in the preceding letter, is used with great appropriateness. He made the work of the ministry the business of his life, and was often heard to say that he viewed the office he held higher than the office of the President of the United States, and that he considered it *a kind of coming down* in the station of the preacher who might think himself *going up* in accepting any civil office within the gift of man. He magnified his office in word and in deed, and always endeavored to elevate the standing and promote the usefulness of his "fellow-helpers to the truth." Cheerfulness, and activity of mind and body were strikingly developed elements in his character. Open-hearted, free, and undissembling in his intercourse with others, he made to himself friends, permanent friends, wherever he went. It is a universal law of our nature to hate hypocrisy in others, though we should be guilty of it ourselves. He was not double-tongued, nor double-faced among his brethren in the gospel ministry, consequently he always had their confidence and hearty co-operation in carrying out the designs of benevolence in which he was so frequently employed. He never sought to promote a good cause by the use of unholy means; nor to correct one evil by the introduction of another. He loved the truth; loved "speaking the truth in love." Probably few men ever excelled him in despising "the sleight of men and cunning craftiness, whereby they lie in wait to deceive."

The Indians loved him more than any other white man who ever preached among them. In proof of this, let another extract from the letter of Elder Webb be introduced. He writes—

"In 1832, at the Tuckasiege Association, on Lord's-day, a considerable number of Cherokees were present, and although the preaching seemed to have a good effect among the white people, the Indians sat unmoved, but kept good order. Some of the young men among them had gone under the stand, and were sitting there quietly, until brother Posey arose to close the services of the day. As soon as they heard *his* voice, most of them arose from their seats and moved forward. The young men came out from under the stand, and all of them looked on with great earnestness. Their countenances indicated that they were excited. They appeared like children receiving the most solemn instructions from a devoted father. I have seen, [says brother Webb,] and conversed with the seals of his ministry among the Cherokees."

To their present homes, in Arkansas, many of them have carried on their tongues the name of Posey, and many have carried in their hearts, through his instrumentality, "the everlasting consolations of a good hope through grace." There is a goodly number of Baptists among the Cherokees.

CHAPTER V.

The organization of the Georgia Baptist Convention.—Presence of Elder Posey.—His labors in Georgia.—Agency for Cave Spring School, in Floyd County.—Death of Mrs. Posey.—His marriage to Mrs. Jane Stokes, and settlement in Newnan.—His death.

HUMPHREY POSEY was a laboring man. His eye, his movement, all indicated he had something to do; and that he felt his was an important work. In June, 1822, while on an agency for Valley Town school, he visited Georgia; and in company with Dr. W. T. Brantly, of Augusta, and Elder Joshua Key, of Burke County, he visited Powelton, and was present at the organization of the Georgia Baptist Convention. The reception he met with from the venerable ministers present on that occasion, may be considered as a good index to the high sense they entertained of his worth, and produced in his bosom a strong attachment to the Baptists of Georgia.

We have said he was a laboring man. His travels in Georgia, the Carolinas, Tennessee, Kentucky, and Missouri, as well as his journeys to Philadelphia, are sufficient evidence of it.

After leaving Valley Town, in 1824, he removed to the old upper counties of Georgia, where he resided for a year or two; and then settled in what is termed the Cherokee country, on a very fertile spot which he designed to make his permanent residence for life. While in this new section of the State, he traveled much, and preached every where he went "the glorious gospel of the blessed God." Being the decided friend of education, he accepted, by the solicitation of the brethren, an agency to procure funds to extricate Hearn Manual Labor School from its then embarrassed condition. It is now relieved and is prosperous; and the place has since become celebrated as the location of the Georgia

Institution for the Education of the Deaf and Dumb.

The extensive acquaintance the subject of this memoir had formed with the Baptists of the United States, and with their great benevolent enterprises, fitted him for any agency in almost any department of labor by which important objects are to be secured. His plans were not visionary, and the means for their accomplishment were well understood by him. From the time he became a citizen of Georgia, he became a regular attendant at the annual meetings of the Georgia Baptist Convention; and such was the respect they had for his opinions, that he was uniformly requested to act on committees of more than ordinary interest to the body. "He was known in the gates when he sat among the elders of the land."

In the providence of God, he was permitted to enjoy the society of the wife of his youth forty-two years. She died at their residence in Walker County, June

22d, 1842. By her he had ten children; eight daughters and two sons, all of whom have given evidence of conversion to God. He was often heard to speak of this as a matter of consolation to him in his declining years. He dedicated his children to God in prayer, daily prayer, which is the only method of dedication about which the Holy Scriptures furnish any instruction. God owned, he hoped, his own method and means of grace, and "sealed with the Holy Spirit of promise" all his children.

On the 28th day of July, 1844, he became united in marriage to Mrs. Jane Stokes, relict of Deacon Wm. M. Stokes, of Newnan, Georgia. He disposed of nearly all his property in Walker county, among his children, and came to Newnan to reside permanently. Several churches in the vicinity called him to preach to them as a pastoral supply, and he devoted his time to their service faithfully, and with much success, up to the close of his life. He was identified with the Baptists in all their benevolent institutions. But the evangelization of the benighted Indians lay nearest his heart, and to the day of his death he was a regular contributor to the funds of the Indian Mission Association. Since his decease, his venerable widow has been a liberal contributor.

Having been appointed at a previous session to preach the missionary sermon before the Western Association, at its meeting in September, 1846, he came forward on the Lord's day, and with much acceptance, performed the service. During his discourse he remarked, he would join any society calculated to do good to his fellow-men. "I would join," said he, "a wolf-killing society, if I lived in a country where wolves were an annoyance." Many Baptists, Methodists, and others, will long remember that last effort of his on the subject of missions. His soul was in the work, he had extraordinary liberty, and probably exerted himself too severely; for in the evening he took a chill, which was followed by high fever. In a few days, however, he was apparently in his usual health. Nevertheless, it was evident that his bodily and mental powers were somewhat enfeebled. Though he attended his churches regularly up to within a few days of his death, yet he seemed to have a kind of presentiment that his days were drawing to a termination. The last sermon he ever delivered was on the second Lord's day in December, at Ebenezer Church, seven miles east of Newnan. He died on the 28th day of December, 1846. Death did not alarm him. Relying on the blood of Jesus Christ to cleanse him from all sin, he felt no fear to "pass through the valley of the shadow of death." Calmly would he converse about it, as his Christian friends came around his bed.

His mortal remains lie seven miles east from Newnan, by the side of those of Deacon W. M. Stokes. His surviving companion has placed over his remains a tomb, covered by a neat marble slab, with the following brief inscription, written by John E. Robinson, Esq.

SACRED

TO THE MEMORY OF
REV. HUMPHREY POSEY,

WHO WAS BORN IN VIRGINIA,

ON THE 12TH OF JANUARY, 1780,

AND DEPARTED THIS LIFE DECEMBER 28TH, 1846.

HE UNITED WITH THE BAPTIST CHURCH

IN 1802, AND WAS, FOR NEARLY HALF A CENTURY,

A FAITHFUL MINISTER OF THE GOSPEL.

> The gospel was his joy and song,
>   E'en to his latest breath;
> The truth he had proclaimed so long,
>   Was his support in death.

By the special request of his son, residing at a distance, Elder Otis Smith, Principal of Brownwood High School, near Lagrange, delivered, in May following, a funeral discourse to a large assemblage of his friends, in the Baptist church at Newnan. The Western Association at its session in September, requested Elder J. E. Dawson to preach a discourse in reference to his memory, to the delegates and friends present. His theme was "*A good minister of Jesus Christ.*" All classes felt that the preacher might give full scope to his feelings with little danger of drawing his picture of a good man too bold and bright.

CHAPTER VI.

Persecution of Elder Posey.—Anecdote.—Method of Preaching.—His portrait.

Jesus Christ told his apostles that in this world they should have tribulation; and Paul at Lystra, Iconium, and Antioch, exhorted the disciples to continue in the faith, declaring that "we must through much tribulation enter into the kingdom of God." Speaking of his fellow-laborers in the work of the ministry, he says, "We are made a spectacle unto the world, and to angels, and to men." 1 Cor., iv. 9. Again, "We are made as the filth of the world and as the offscouring of all things unto this day." "Blessed are ye," says Christ, "when men shall revile you, and persecute you, and shall say all manner of evil against you, falsely, for my sake." This blessing came upon our venerable brother Posey. "Remember," said Jesus, "the word that I said unto you, the servant is not greater than his Lord. If they have persecuted me, they will also persecute you." The cause of all this is revealed in another place in holy writ, and deserves special notice. "*The wicked watcheth the righteous, and seeketh to slay him. The Lord will not leave him in his hand, nor condemn him when he is judged.*" Ps. xxxvii. 32, 33. Elder Posey had his enemies, his trials, his troubles, and his persecution. He could not have been a minister of Jesus Christ without them. It may be proper to give an extract from a letter from Deacon James Whitaker. He writes as follows:—

"*Valley Town, Jan.* 9, 1849.
DEAR BROTHER,—

You ask me for a sketch of the character of Elder Humphrey Posey. I have known him upwards of forty years. I saw him ordained to the ministry forty-three years ago next May. Like most other good men, the shafts of the wicked were sometimes hurled at him, but always fell harmless at his feet.

He was a very poor man, with a rising family, when he commenced the ministry. He preached successfully, and taught school for the support of his family. His character as a teacher and a minister stood high. He was cheerful and friendly in his intercourse with mankind. His mind was well stored with anecdote.

He was once attacked by a poltroon, who was on a circuit, bearing the name of a preacher, in which case a suit was brought, when the character of Posey came through unscathed, while the name of the other stands on the records of the court, branded with falsehood."

Is it not a great blessing that though *"the wicked watcheth the righteous and seeketh to slay him."* yet *"the Lord will not leave him in his hand, nor condemn him when he is judged?"* This is a source of peculiar consolation to the man of God, who in this world "SHALL HAVE TRIBULATION."

That Elder Posey's mind should be "well stored with anecdote," is not surprising, when it is remembered that he was nearly all his life traveling and preaching among almost all classes of his fellow-men. That he was extraordinarily gifted in applying an anecdote is very well known by those who were intimately acquainted with him. The writer of this sketch having known him ever since the organization of the Georgia Baptist Convention, which occurred in June, 1822, remembers particularly his very pertinent application of the following; and the cases in which it might be applied are so numerous, that an insertion of it can scarcely be considered out of place in this brief Memoir. I shall give it as I find it now in print, though Elder Posey related it, *in his own words*, to a fireside circle of brethren, in which the conversation was respecting the causes of frequent changes of pastors in the churches. It is as follows:—

" The people in one of the out parishes

in Virginia wrote to Dr. Rice, who was then at the head of the Theological Seminary, in Prince Edward, for a minister. They said they wanted a man of *first rate talents*, for they had run down considerably, and needed building up. They wanted one who could *write well*, for some of the young people were very nice about *that matter*. They wanted one who could *visit* a good deal, for their former minister had neglected *that*, and they wanted to *bring it up*. They wanted a man of very GENTLEMANLY DEPORTMENT, for some thought a great deal of *that*. And so they went on, describing a perfect minister. The last thing they mentioned was—they gave their last minister three hundred and fifty dollars; but if the Doctor would send them such a man as they had described, they would raise another fifty dollars, making it four hundred. The Doctor sat right down and wrote a reply, telling them that they ought forthwith to make a CALL for old Doctor Dight, in heaven; for he did not know any one in *this world* who answered their description. And as Dr. Dwight had been living so long on spiritual food, he might not need so much for the body, and possibly he might live on four hundred dollars."

Dr. Franklin, the great American philosopher, often carried his point in an argument by the introduction of an appropriate anecdote. Mr. Posey related anecdotes in the social circle with great ease, appropriateness and effect, yet he seldom introduced them to illustrate any thing in his pulpit performances. He could enjoy himself pleasantly in the parlor, in an easy and familiar strain of conversation, and rarely failed to render others easy and pleasant in his company. But when he entered the pulpit, he was grave—he was solemn.— "Thou, God, seest me," seemed to influence his whole life; but especially in the pulpit he appeared never to forget it. He could not pardon any thing like witticism in the sacred desk. He never took a "quip or merry turn."

As respects his course in the pastoral care of the churches he served, it was a uniform rule with him to resign, whenever he discovered his opinions and feelings were not respected as he conceived they should be. Always sustaining with dignity the Moderator's chair, he scarcely ever failed to secure from his brethren a respectful and dignified address in the business of conference. "Let all things be done decently and in order" was his motto on all occasions. When this is adhered to by the Pastor, there is despatch in the affairs which usually come before the conference, and there is secured a decent respect for the character of the church from the world.

In reference to his dress—his apparel— it might not be amiss to state, for the benefit of the rising ministry of the present age, that he was very plain and prudent in his clothing. Like the departed Luther Rice, he had too much to do, his heart was too much set on doing it, and his time was too precious to be wasted in attention to such matters. He placed very little value upon fashionable gloves or fine coats. His towering mind rose above the region in which such things are thought of most.

With regard to his sermons, it is a remarkable fact, that though a good penman, he never wrote a sermon during his long and very acceptable ministerial course; and among his papers I do not find even a skeleton of a sermon. And yet his discourses were generally well-arranged, systematical, and full of good sense, containing clear and forcible exhibitions of Bible truth. He pursued, through life, a course of theological studies, which, it is feared, is greatly neglected by many of the young as well as old ministers of the present day. He studied the Bible closely, and was mighty in the English version of the scriptures. In this respect his tongue was "the pen of a ready writer." He considered "*Faith the starting point and moving power of the divine life;*" repentance, fear, hope, love, are but its works. It must, therefore, itself be the divine work it is said to be; and though divine, it is, on our part, the simplest and first of all good works. His religious creed was not a heterogeneous, absurd mass of indefinable opinions; but it was clearly conceived, well digested, and fully sustained in his sermons.

He was a great admirer of the late Dr. Wm. Staughton, the author of the Abridgment of Gill's Body of Divinity, and the reputed mover of, and assistant in, the organization of the first Female Bible Society in the world. With the Doctor, during his engagement at Valley Town, he carried on a regular and very interesting correspondence; and many of his letters were published, particularly those giving an account of his labors as missionary among the Indians. Dr. S. esteemed him very highly, for his work's sake; and his family were uncommonly warm in their attachment to him. And when at Philadelphia, on the duties of his agency, a daughter of that distinguished man of God, being skilled in portrait painting, requested him to sit, that she might transmit his interesting features to the canvas. He complied with this request, and she took, it is said, a very accurate likeness, which was afterwards presented to the Columbian College, at Washington city, where it may probably be still seen.

Mrs. Posey, ample in her resources, and long well known as a liberal Baptist, still living, and ready to every good work, procured, at her own expense, the beautiful engraving which accompanies these pages. She had it made from a daguerreotype likeness. It will be easy to discover from his portrait that he was an interesting man. Decision and promptitude, firmness and inflexibility of purpose, for which he was so remarkable, are very distinctly developed in his features.

She had a likeness, large as life, painted from the same daguerreotype, a year or more after his death. When the artist had finished his work, he invited the friends of Elder Posey to call at Dr. J. W. Terrell's residence, in Newnan, where it was placed in the parlor, that they might see it. Numbers, feeling anxious to have such a privilege, went. The painting was placed in a frame with the face to the wall, and when the friends were seated, according to his wishes, he turned it to their view. Such was the effect produced, that some wept. This is stated, not to praise the unnamed artist for his skill, but to let the reader know that Elder Humphrey Posey lives in the recollection of the people of Newnan, and lives; it is believed, in everlasting remembrance before God in heaven.

THE END.

www.ingramcontent.com/pod-product-compliance
Lightning Source LLC
Chambersburg PA
CBHW070621050426
42450CB00011B/3097